A Biography of the Bookcase on my Side of the Bed

David Macpherson

A Biography of the Bookcase on my Side of the Bed

1

The Bookcase

My wife got it for me to get the books off the floor. They had been gathering there with the plan to read them next, or the next after that. Whenever. The books were meant to be read. Now they were in piles by the window sill like ancient burial mounds.

She told me this would be good for all the recent books.

It was a thoughtful gift. It certainly was going to make it easier to walk on that side of the room.

It had three shelves. It was three quarters full as soon as I got it and started removing the books from the floor and putting it there.

This was in 2020, in the early months of the Pandemic season.

I kept on buying books like I always did.

I was not reading as quickly. Even though I was home a lot more, I was watching things on the internet instead of my first love, reading.

And even with the awareness of that, I kept on buying books.

After a year or two, I could not put put anymore books on the shelves. They were tight and teaming.

The books started piling up on the floor. Like before. As if the floof by the window missed the weight of all those unread books. The floor was lonely.

I still intend to read them. Most of the books there have not been even attempted. But that's good. That's a good reason for a bookshelf. In a Harlan Ellison story, someone asks an old man if he read all those books he has on his bookshelf. The reply was, "Hell no. Why would I want a bookshelf with books I already read?"

With that in mind, I have made this bookshelf very happy. Ready to take up its responsibility. These are the books you want to read. These are the books you got from various bookshops or loved ones who gave them to you because they were sure you would dig it. These are those books. The perfect bookshelf. For me.

It is filled with crime novels and treatises on fairy tales and graphic novels and comics. There are a lot of comics.

This is the history of my interests. This is a history of buying and reading books during and after the pandemic. This is everything you need to know about me. The first thing you can realize about me is that I don't read as much as I used to.

The Top Shelf
From Left to Right

The Hungry Tiger of Oz by Ruth Plumly Thompson. This is a Del Rey paperback that I bought for 3 dollars from a West Hartford bookstore called Brick Walk Books. This was a cramped and very good used bookstore that had original art in between the shelves. I was there once and he and another guy were talking about an art exhibit that the store owner helped put together for the New Britain Museum of American Art. This was kind of exciting for me. It had all my favorite things: books and art. I sought out this bookstore because it was written about in a memoir about book collecting called Used and Rare by Laurence and Nancy Goldstone. They wrote three books about collecting books in New England and I made it a thing to go to the stores they mentioned. This one figured highly in their books. I went there a few times and spoke to the owner. He said that for a while, he did not sell online and he regrets the years of selling he missed on. He also said that he keeps a brick and mortar store so that people can find him to sell him books. I bought this and the next two books around 2017 or so. Around 2018, I went back there and there was the sign that read, "Closed for Renovations." I have seen that very sign on favorite book stores and restaurants before and that always meant, "We are out of business but not ready to admit it to ourselves yet." The next time I was around there, the storefront was now an antique store.

The Gnome King of Oz by Ruth Plumly Thompson. Another Del Rey book in great shape that I got from Brick Walk Books for three bucks. I didn't read any of the Oz books until I was in my twenties. I missed the right years to discover them. I read a handful of the Baum books. I also got into the silent Oz movies that Baum directed himself. Ruth Plumly

Thompson was the next Oz writer after Baum died. She was a writer for the children's section of a Philadelphia newspaper and was excellent. I had a book of her newspaper stories and I thought it was great. So I was very excited to find these. Getting her books were never as easy as finding the original fourteen books that Baum wrote. These are very nice paperbacks with lovely painted covers by Michael Herring (I never heard of him, but the covers are cool.) Because there is one more of these Oz books on the shelf, I will stop here and move on to the next book.

Grampa in Oz by Ruth Plumly Thompson. Del Rey. Three bucks from the same place. Great shape. I never read these books. They have stayed for almost a decade in the bedroom because I have always intended to read them. I started one of them but it never struck me. I always figured I would get back to them. Though I love the American style fairy tales of the Oz books, they can be a little tough to read for me. They are too episodic for me to dive into them one after the other. Dorothy and Ozma and the gang go to one new territory with weird creatures and have a small adventure and then on to the next territory and the next until the story is done. It seemed that the Thompson ones had the same structure and I have not really found myself invested in getting back to them. They are staying on the shelf, because I want to read them. I want to be amazed and astounded by a hundred year old fantasy.

Trek by Samuel C. Gaskin This is a self-produced graphic novel. It is 48 pages which can count as a graphic novel in some parts. It is stapled like a comic, though smaller. Sam is a distant friend. He was a kid in the poetry scene in which I was part of Worcetster. He wrote very strange and very funny pieces. He also was a comic artist. I think I picked this up not from him but from the "Local Artists" section of the main comic shop in town. I want to think it cost me three or five dollars. I have read this and it was a strange quest fantasy. He drew the whole thing in sharpie. I love when people I know create. I love to see their unexpected artistry. I knew Sammy as a teenage slam poet. Then he was making weird, funny comics. The last time I saw him he was part of a show of noise artists. His work was engaging and not as off putting as I thought it would be. He is now married with children. I like seeing these old comics he created to remind me that there are worlds of creativity in our little towns and little circles.

Sugarcube by Samuel C. Gaskin. Another graphic novel (this one 72 pages) that is self made and stapled like a comic. This one I remember reading when I bought it from Sam. I think it was five bucks. This is a great little book. It deals with the Sam character discovering he has diabetes and how he handled it all. This is one of those times I get annoyed that certain books are self made and slightly distributed. This is actually a very heartfelt and odd look at illness. I want to recommend it to many people, but how many copies are out there? I consider myself lucky that I have it and read it, but I am also saddened by all the others who might get something from this who doesn't even know it exists. I don't know why this book and the previous one are on this bookshelf. In our attic, we have a large box filled with zines and comics and chapbooks from the years we attended open mic poetry events. These two books spent a long time in that box. For some reason I rescued them from the attic and now they are sequestered in the bookcase. I might put them back in the box to have room for another book, a book I have not yet read and know that I already love.

How to Read a Novelist by John Freeman. My wife got me this. I love to read about authors and figure out what they do well. This is a survey of a bunch of writers. The sticker is still on the book and lets me know that she got it for $7.98. THis is one I think I would like to read, but just never have gotten too. I keep forgetting I have it. That will probably be a running theme of this survey. There will be a few times where I will say, "Oh yeah, that book." The problem is that I keep getting new books and the ones already present get pushed to the side. If they don't get read right away, their chances of being consumed decrease.

Savage Gods by Paul Kingsnorth. My wife got this for me a few years ago. I started reading it but only got a few pages. I remember not completely gelling with the prose style. But Heather got it for me on one of her travels and it is a hell of a good looking book and it is a memoir of the challengings of being a writer. It deserves to be tried again. Maybe that's why it has persisted on the nearby bookshelf. The look of the book is awesome and it should stay probably just for aesthetics alone. If I bought it myself, I probably would have already given up on it, but this was a gift and books given as a kindness always deserve multiple attempts.

Waldo and Magic, Inc. by Robert Heinlein. This book was loaned to me by my friend Bob a while ago. Maybe a dozen years ago. Oh man, I am the worst friend. I have never been a big Robert Heinlein fan. Bob, though, loves Heinlein. He has a bookcase filled with Heinlein paperbacks. Before the Pandemic, a group of friends would gather at Bob's every Saturday for a nice meal and good company. I must have seen this book at one of those evenings and asked him if I could give it a try. I recall hearing that his short novel, Magic, Inc, was a clever story and I wanted to give it a shot. I hate the idea that I am one of those friends who don't return books lent to them. Or that I return them in lousy condition. I have lent out books I adore to friends, with the unexamined knowledge that they won't give them back. Is that just part of the book lover's existence? Do we lend out books like some deep seated faith that we test over and over? I didn't read much of it. According to the bookmark, I started with Magic, Inc and only got about ten pages into it. I have a vague memory of digging it. But I guess I didn't dig it enough to finish it. I stopped after writing this sentence and texted Bob to let him know that the book is still with me and ask him if he wanted it back. He replied, "If you haven't read it yet, then you should keep it until you do. If you have lost interest then I'll accept it back at some point. I haven't missed it, though it would be fun to reread at some point." What a wonderful friend. I texted that I will keep it for a bit longer and this time, I am going to read Magic, Inc. Wish me luck.

The Last Selchie Child by Jane Yolen. I read this one when my wife gave it to me ten years ago. I love Jane Yolen. I have a good deal of her books. This book was signed by Ms Yolen, but it was already signed when my wife picked it up. She had a small press at the time and went to a large publishing event in Boston. Midsummer Night's Press was there with this and other books. Heather is good at getting me Yolen books. Why is this book on this bookshelf? I think it hid there. It is a very small book, something like three by five inches. It can easily get lost. When I pulled it just now to write about it, I was surprised it was there. Not unhappily surprised, just amazed that it has not gotten totally lost. Little books have a way of hiding too well.

Book Signing 101: An Author's Guide by Rob Watts. This was purchased in a bookstore in Wolfeboro, New Hampshire at a lovely independent bookstore, The Country Bookseller. The family went there in October of 2020. My wife was feeling restless during the second half of that first Pandemic year. She got us hotel rooms in a variety of places during this time. We would be somewhere else in a hotel room, mostly staying by ourselves. But it wasn't our house. It was a new place with new things to see. One of them was this lovely town. My son and I walked down to the bookstore and it was great. He got a book about politics, because what 13 year old doesn't want a book about modern politics. I got a few things, but I saw this in the used section and something about it made me want it. It had a few things that made me want to pick it up. First, it was 2.98. A cheap book is a small gamble. There are few risks to a cheap book. The second thing is that the font on the book is huge. It is almost in Large Print territory. And my eyes like that thing. I don't like to admit it, but reading has become harder as my eyes get wearier. The last thing was that I had been writing these little Bad Writer's Guides that mocked all the advice given to writers. I had written four or five of them that year and I figured that this book would give me the template to write the Bad Writer's Guide to Book Signings. But I only read a little of the book before something else got my attention and then I kind of got sick of writing the Bad Writer's Guides. So the book has languished. But I love reading advice books for writers, so I will give it a shot somewhere down the line.

Collected Monologues by Charles Cros. I read this. I had a good time with this. Why is this on the bookshelf? Am I going to go back to it and read it some more? This was published by one of my favorite small presses, Black Scat Books. I have been published in a few of their anthologies, but that's not why I like them so. They put out a lot of the absurdist French writers from the 1890s. These guys were really doing something. I knew Charles Cros because Edward Gorey turned one of Cros's pieces into an illustrated book. That's why I got this particular one and it was fun. I used a few of the monologues as intro pieces when I ran a poetry reading. Charles Cros fit in well with open mic poetry apparently. Every six months or so I get the need for weird writings and will order a book from Black Scat. WIth these books I read them and then put them into the small free lending libraries around town. It amuses me to put these books in those little boxes filled with summer romance novels. That's probably what I should do with this book. It's great, but it is also great to send it out in the world. The stranger the book, the better it is out in the wild.

The Essential New York Times Book of Cocktails edited by Steve Redicliffe My mother got this for me as a gift during Christmas. I was in the process of doing a blog project where I would go to every bar in the city of Worcester, have a gin and tonic and write about it. She figured I would like to know about the wonderful world of cocktails in general. I have always loved cocktail culture, maybe a little too much. I don't drink anymore, but the book is still this amazing rock. It is teeming with recipes for cocktails, but better yet are essays about certain cocktails. It's a book to dip into. This is not one to plow through in a sitting or two. This is to pick up and find something tantalizing. Does my relationship to a book like change now that I am no longer drinking? You bet. But in the past this book might have been a to-do list of drinks to try, now it is a warm piece of nostalgia, where I would say to, "I used to love that kind of drink while sitting in that special place at the end of the bar."

Tom Petty: Essays on the Life and Work Edited by Crystal D. Sands. One of my writing projects in the fall of 2019 was to write about a a music video second by second. Each short chapter was one second of the video. I randomly picked a Tom Petty video, "You Got Lucky." It took months to write the eighteen thousand words of the book. (It is called In This Reality, if you are interested, but no big deal either way.) I guess all my friends knew of this project and all that it was ridiculous. I have liked Tom Petty, but he has never been a big one for me. I think I bought one of his CDs once. But for a little while, I was known as a Tom Petty freak.

My wife went to an academic press convention and she picked this book up for me. I believe I read one or two of these essays. They are very set in the series ways of academic writing, where there is deep meaning in the fun rock songs. I am fascinated with the idea of academic writing, where they better be writing dense articles about pop culture or they might lose their jobs. It is wild. I don't know if I will get back to this book, but it was a kind gift. Those are ones that stay on the shelf longer than the ones I buy for myself.

The Kick-Ass Writer by Chuck Wendig I read his blog and some of his novels. He is a good writer and his take on writing is realistic and funny. I don't know why I have not read this book cover to cover because I like him. I have dipped into this on occasion. I got this from Barnes and Noble. I haunt the Writing Reference section. I am always looking for the book that will have the key that will finally unlock my skills as a writer. I know. Nonsense. But it can't hurt to try.

Hark! The Herald Angels Scream edited by Christopher Golden. This was a Christmas present from my wife. It has a great creepy cover. It has a bunch of awesome writers. I think I began to read this in the first few weeks of the Pandemic. I was taking my dog for insanely long walks and reading books at the same time. Fitzy was slowing down and it made reading much easier. Reading Christmas horror stories seemed fine for a warm Spring. I only read two stories. The first story was good. The second one was good too, but I hated the ending of it so much. The main characters accidentally get their small child killed. I can see how the story was leading to that moment, but I hated that. I hate writing about it now. I am not putting down the story, but the way my head was during those lock-down days didn't want to read such dire things. I put it on the shelf and it stayed there. Will I like the other stories or should I not even dare?

The book remains, a silent reminder that other stories might entertain, might wash the bad taste out of my mouth.

The Portable Henry Rollins by Henry Rollins. This is a reference book for me. I will read it when I decide it is time. I had an idea to write a book about traveling rock musicians on a low budget tour. I have read about that life in zines, but I felt that I really needed to know more. I recalled Henry Rollins had a tour diary book called Get in the Van. This was in my head when I went back in 2018 to a used bookstore in Narragansett, Rhodes Island. I was wandering around and this book appeared. I looked and it had 20 pages from Get in the Van. Not the whole book, but good enough. I bought it for eight dollars. I still intend to write that book so I guess I should keep this volume around. In case of creative emergency, break glass.

The Complete Blammo Volume One by Noah Van Sciver. This volume contains issues one through five of blammo with some additional comments and comics. This is when the comics and graphic novels really start to show up on the shelf. They were already there, but there is a ton of comics on these shelves and this is where it truly begins. Noah Van Sciver puts out his personal one person anthology called Blammo. I think there have been eleven of them over the decades. I like his work. I remember seeing some strange strips he did in Mad Magazine. What made me a big fan was through comic video watching on YouTube during the pandemic. He would interview other alternative cartoonists and I enjoyed those conversations. Just because I am not a comic creator doesn't mean I am not going to get something useful from then. Creation is creation and it is always necessary to learn from others. In some of the videos he would show what he was working on and tell us how to pick up his work. That's fair. This was part of a Kickstarter campaign for Kilgore

Press. I don't know how much I spent, maybe 35 or something, because I also picked up another book they put out (coming next) for that. I poured over this when I got it. I particularly enjoyed reading his notes on the process. But I guess I never read all the comics. The thing is with this book, these are early works. The first few issues are not as polished in writing or art than what he makes now, or even made a decade ago. Early work can be tough. I know I will sit down one day and finish it. I like how deals with the personal as well as the historical in his work.

My Hot Date (and other embarrassments) by Noah Van Sciver. This came with the Complete Blammo. This is a collection of his pieces about being a poor teenager in the 90s. I like the art a lot, but I might not have tried it because stories about kids getting embarrassed and doing cringey things is not a favorite of mine. I know I want to read it, but I guess I have to be in a brave, determined mood to tackle it. This is a 64 page comic that has staples instead of a spine, and I have an issue with that. I know it is cheaper to do it that way, but at 64 pages, I want this to have a spine and be a book on the shelf and not a comic book that has stolen its way on the shelf with all the other books. I don't need unity on my bookshelves, I just think this little collection would be happier as a full book with a spine.

The Nib Volumes 4 through 15 edited by Matt Bors. Each of these 100 page anthologies contains comics journalism. This came from the Nib, which was an online daily site for political cartooning and cartoon journalism. I would go there every now and then. In 2019, the company that they were part of ended their funding on the Nib. The Nib went out on their own and looked for people to subscribe. I did. As part of the subscription, they sent out these quarterly Nib issues. Each one had a theme like Scams, Drugs, Pandemic and Cities. I have read much of it and there are a few issues I devoured. They are on the shelf as a reminder of independent reporting and publishing. I dig having them as a large group. They look handsome there on the top shelf. They are good to read too. Can't forget that.

Lou by Melissa Mendes. I have supported writers and artists in their desire to make their work. One of the way I supported comic creators was by subscribing to Oily Comics. Oily Comics made little mini comics. Mini comics are three by five inches and these were around sixteen pages. If you subscribed monthly you would get a handful of brand new mini comics. One of the mini series was The End of the Fucking World, which became a Netflix series. Another series that I got from the Oily subscription was Lou. It showed the life of a tomboy who gets involved in some criminal activity in her rural town. I loved it. It was great. But I started my subscription when it was at issue five and I didn't renew the subscription after six months, so I never got the end of the story. I found out that Mendes got the whole book published, so I had my local comic shop order it. It cost fifteen dollars. It was a great story. I really like it. I might give the book away. I really love it but I don't think I will reread it and I want to share it with others. By the time I am done with this brief biography this book might be out there in the world, looking for another person to love it.

A Woman's Walk - Compiled by the London Library. This is a part of a series of little books that the Pushkin Press does where the London Library comes up with a theme and then they scour their archive for interesting pieces of writing that fits that theme. The series is called "Found on the Shelves," which is funny because all of the books I am writing it found on the shelves. Mine is more broadly focused. Here, this book is about the Victorian trend of women taking long walks in nature. This little book contains about ten excerpts about women in the outdoors. I haven't gotten to it. Whenever I see any books in this series, I buy them. That means these tiny volumes are scattered about the house's bookcases to be ready whenever I get in the right mood for Victorian non-fiction.

Do The Right Thing by Ed Guerrero. This is a monograph, whatever that is exactly.. It is a book about the Spike Lee movie, which I love. My wife got this for me a few years back. Haven't gotten to it. I bet you that the next time I watch the movie, I will search for this book and give it a shot. It is always a good idea to salt the house with a variety of books and ideas, so when you want to explore something, all you need to do is scour the shelves and there it will be.

The Wicked Go To Hell by Frederic Dard. There are a few French crime writers that I love. They are dark and mean and it is all very cool. Simenon, when not writing about Maigret, did a bunch of these ugly little books. I say ugly in the best way. Heather and I were in New York, going to museums, and stopped at the Corner Bookshop in the Upper East Side. It was a great bookstore. They had these books by Dard that Pushkin Press put out. I never heard of him but the cover was cool. Over the years, I picked up a couple other books by Dard. I don't know if it is me or the books, but I have not been able to finish any of them. They are short books, so I have a hope that I will be able to plow through them. This collection of books seems to have the theme of hope. I hope to read it later. I hope that I was just in a bad mood when I started the book. I hope that all books will make me happy and whole.

Brooklyn by Wildsam Field Guides. My wife got it for me. I was born in Brooklyn. I bore her with stories of spending time with my grandmother in Brooklyn. I never lived in Brooklyn, but I obnoxiously claim it as my own. She gave me this funny field guide. I have not given it enough time. It is hanging out on the shelf until I do.

Vanish by Paavan Buddhdev. This was on Kickstarter. It struck me as something I might like to read, so I supported the campaign. It took a while before it came. The book is a lovely thing. It arrived with postcards and errata. The errata states, "Thank you for getting a copy of this Kickstarter edition of my book Vanish. In the book, I explore what it means to make something disappear. However, I wrote the bulk of this before the pandemic really started to affect our lives. Looking over it now, there's so much more that could have been said about things that have changed, things that have disappeared. I hope you and your loved ones are safe." The author is a self identified magician, so disappearing as a topic is perfect for him. But I didn't gell with the text when I tried it.

Born to Weird by Set Sytes. In the last entry and many others, I have said I have not gelled with the writing and put it down. In this one, I have not read one word. I bought it at the Book Loft in Great Barrington, Massachusetts because the cover has tentacles on it and I am a sucker for horror books with tentacles on the covers. It was in the fifty percent off shelf so I paid 6.50 for the book. The book I have not even attempted to read.

Email by Randy Malamud. It turns out that I have history with this book. I didn't know it when I bought it. I got it from a wonderful Connecticut bookstore called R.J. Julia. You should check it out. They have a great little cafe attached that my son is partial to. This is part of the Bloomsvbury series called Object Lessons. They are single topic books about objects that we encountered. There are books in the series such as, Cigarette Lighter, Hotel Room, Bookshelf and many others. I love small books that have one subject. I think there will be a few more books like that on the shelf. The object in this one is a look at how we use email. I thought it fascinating. I showed the book to Heather and she was taken about. She spent a few months trying to find the right Ph.D. program for her to take and one of the people she focused on was Randy Malamud. She went down to Atlanta to meet him. She read a bunch of his books. Though she was accepted into the program, there was no student aid for it, so she had to pass on it. To see me pick up a book by a guy she tried to be a student of was a little weird for her. I started the book and it was good, but I got distracted with other books. Other things. Other objects to be given lessons from.

Art Afterpieces by Ward Kimball. Owning a copy of this book was the end result of a lengthy rabbit hole I fumbled down one afternoon. I was writing a zine about an oversized comic book that Wammo put out in the 60s. It was two and a half feet tall and sold in toy stores. It had to have a lot of comics to fill all those oversized pages. One of the strips in the comic was by Ward Kimball. As part of the zine/book that I was writing, I did a little bio on each of the artists. Ward Kimball was one of the great Disney animators. He then went to do TV specials about space. This book was a popular one, done in 1970. He took classic pieces of art and added them to it. So Whistler' mother is watching TV. The Boy Blue had a goatee and sunglasses. The Gaugan still life of oranges has the word Suncist stamped on the oranges. That kind of thing. I ordered a cheap copy through Amazon when I heard of it. I got it and looked at it. It is cute. It is kind of funny. I can let it go. It just doesn't make me smile as much as I thought it would.

Forgotten Journey by Silvina Ocampo. This book is here to remind me that I really need to read her work. She was part of the literary scene with Jorge Luis Borges in Argentina. She was married to the amazing writer Adolfo Boiy Casares. I have read a strange mystery book that she and her husband created, but I have not read the stories she is most known for. I have a great love for these writers. For the longest time, I didn't even own a copy of her work. One time in Putney Vermont, I went into a beautiful shop called Antidote Books where I encountered a table filled with enticing offerings. I saw this and knew I needed it. I have not tried to read it, but I will. That's not a false promise. That is something I know I have to do.

OK Computer by Dai Griffiths. This is part of another wonderful series of small books that focus on just one thing. This series is 33 ⅓ and each book is about one important album. It mostly talks of the album's influence and how it was created. I have many of the books in this series. I don't even have to know the album to want to read it. I don't know when I bought this book. I don't know why I have it. I mean, I had the Radiohead album this is about, and I mostly liked it, but I still don't know why this is one of the books from the series that makes its home in my bedroom. Maybe that's why I haven't even tried to read it.

Steady Rollin': Preacher's Kids, Black Punk and Pedaling Papa by Fred Noland. This is a comic book memoir about biking. I guess it is also about punk, which is cool. I don't know much about it. I got it as part of a kickstarter for the season's slate from Bird Cage Bottom Books. They would always put out interesting comics. I tended to get four books for my backing payment. This came last year. I am so curious about this. I can't wait to get to it. I love getting multiple books from small press publishers doing crowdfunding. There is always something to be surprised by. Always something that you might love.

\

What is the Grass: Walt Whitman in My life by Mark Doty. My wife loves Mark Doty. When we were first seeing each other, we would read to each other in the car. I remember she read one of his books during a long car trip. We saw Doty read when he just published his book Dog Days. I discovered that he wrote about his love of Walt Whitman. I love Walt Whitman. I thought this would be great to jump into. I honestly thought that Heather giving me a copy would force me to stop whatever I was reading and dive deep into this. After a few pages, I was reminded that Mark Doty is not someone you read casually. His language is difficult and beautiful. I put it on the bookshelf. I have to admit that I forgot that I have this book.

For Your Consideration: Dwayne The Rock Johnson by Tres Dean. This was a series of books where they take fun, but not serious actors, and create a very serious book about them. During the early days of the Pandemic, when Barnes and Noble was open again, I saw two of these books and bought them. I read the one about Keanu Reaves and thought it was funny, though a little forced. I decided that I would take a break before reading this one. And now we are here, four years later. I wish I was a fast reader. I wish it was as easy to read a book as it is to buy one. I will read this during a moment when I need silly stupid books. I have a lot of books that fit that bill.

Embracing the Burlesque of Collateral Damage by Richard Fox. This one hurts. It hurts because I have not read it. It hurts because Richard was a friend who died last year. He spent most of the time I knew him refusing to succumb to brain cancer. That man was so fierce. ANd kind. And a hell of a poet. He was a regular at the poetry reading

I ran. I was so happy when he read. I always let him read as long as he wants. Sometimes, others would complain that I let him go past the time limit but no one else. I would tell them that it is Richard and he gets to read as long as he damn well wants. Besides, we would not be able to hear him forever. He was also a generous audience member who seemed to love everything he heard. He was the kind of poet and writer I hope to be. These poems make a long narrative. He gave this to me when it was published. He was kind enough to give me copies of all his books. This has a dedication on the title page. "Dave - Thanks for making a community. These were first shouted on your stage. Love - Richard." I was crying while writing that. Maybe that's why I haven't read it yet. I can't read the dedication without crying, how the hell will I get through the whole book. You should read his work. He was a hine poet. And so lovely.

The Black Lizard and Beast in the Shadows by Edogawa Rampo. There is a lot to say about this book. A book I have not read. I first heard of Rampo in the late 90s. I saw a trailer for a movie called The Mystery of Rampo. It looked like a cool Japanese period flick. When it came on video I watched it and it was okay. It was about a mystery writer in the 1920s. Only later did I learn that Rampo was one of the most important Japanese writers of horror and mystery. Over the next two decades, I would look for books by him and never find them. My curiosity was piqued. In 2017, I started the habit of going to Brattleboro Vermont for a writing weekend. It was a great little town filled with art and bookstores. It turns out that the location really was conducive for my writing. It is just a place that works for me. And there are a lot of bookstores. On the first day I ever was in Brattleboro, I went into a shop called Mystery on Main. he sold nothing but mystery books. He had mystery books from the most obscure of publishers. This place was amazing. And on that day, I looked in the R section for Rampo and this book was there. I almost giggled to myself. Here was Rampo. The guy from the movie from twenty years ago. I couldn't buy that book faster than I did. This has two of his novellas. I just haven't gotten to it. Last year, at Barnes and Noble, there was a Rampo book. I bought that one too. I read a few of the stories in that book and Rampo is wonderfully creepy. This stays near me on this shelf because I will read this one day. Mystery on Main closed in 2018, the owner retired. I am sad by that, but in some ways it is good because I spent so much money there. There are other books on the shelf that I got there, so I will be talking of that much missed place again.

Daily Rituals: How Artists Work by Mason Curry. I have only owned this book for a month. I was pissed off at work. A co-worker really upset me and I left work angry. Before I headed home I knew I had to chill out. I went to Barnes and Noble and wandered around the stacks, looking for something that would make me feel less annoyed. After thirty minutes, I found nothing I might want. I was getting even more pissed. Then I saw this book in the Art section. It is a compilation of writers, artists and creative types and how they made their art. I bought it and got home and read the first few pages. I felt immersed by the stories of how the writers I admire create their routines to create their work. After that, I put it on the bookshelf, knowing that I will get to it when I am upset again. I am sure I won't have too long to wait.

Hawks of the Seas by Will Eisner. Discovering the work of Will Eisner at the age of 12 changed me as a reader. Not just as a reader of comic books but as a reader in general. I used to hang out at my town's comic book shop for hours on end. That allowed me to find interesting comics. One of them were reprints of the Spirit comics from the 1940s. They were made by Will Eisner and I loved them. Throughout my adolescence I read the Spirit reprints and Eisner's more recent work. In 1978, he put out A Contract with God, that many call the first graphic novel. It was not, but it still has that title. This is a collection of swashbuckling strips he made in 1940, before the Spirit. I knew of them, but never owned a collection or read them. A few years ago, there was a large antique mall in Rhode Island that was having a giant 50 cent comic sale. They had thousands of comics and over several weeks I would go and pick up great comics for cheap. I went one afternoon after work, hoping to pick up more fifty cent comics, but they were all gone. The sale was over and there were no more comics. I was bummed. I wandered around the huge building and found a section of discount graphic novels. I went through it as a consolation prize. I saw this book and realized I should own it. It was five dollars. The art is nice and I have spent time admiring it but have not gotten around to reading it. The text is small and my eyes don't like that. I figure when I finally break down and buy a very bright lamp that will allow me to read small type better that I will get to it.

Middle Shelf
Reading from Left to Right

Henry Speaks for Himself by John Liney. Henry was a comic strip character with no hair and never spoke. He was in all the funny pages. I don't think it was anybody's favorite. It was very safe and when you think of the bald, silent kid, you would have to admit it was pretty weird. I was in a new bookstore in Worcester, Bedlam Books. It is a used and remaindered bookstore. They didn't have a graphic novel section at the time, but had some on a window sill in the back of the store. This was here and I was shocked to see that it reprinted Henry comic book stories from the fifties. I was mostly shocked because Henry spoke in them. It was 5.95 so I bought it. I read half of it and it is a very odd experience. The storytelling is off. They say that in good stories, things are causal. This happens because that happened. In these stories, there was nothing connected. One thing happened and then another thing happened and then another thing, with no relationship to each other. Henry would narrate adventures around town and things just occurred. It is a wild way to tell a story. I liked it, but it was tiring. I put it on the shelf and have not gotten back to it. But the storytelling is worth revisiting. Who knew that I would find something worthwhile in a Henry comic. Wonders never cease.

Bad Stories: How the Hell Did We Get Here by Steve Almond. This was one of my books of tithing. It is how I think of a book I buy when I am at a nice book shop but can't find anything I am desperate to own and take home to read right away but instead I just buy something of possible interest because I like the store and it deserves to have people buy things. That is how I got this book. I was in Jeff Kinney's bookstore in Plainville Ma and I liked the store and couldn't leave empty handed. Jeff Kinney is the author of the Diary of a Wimpy Kid books and he opened up a really nice bookshop. It is a great place, but for some reason, nothing was singing to me. No book was begging to be taken home. We were there for an hour and my son found a few books. I looked in different sections, feeling the pressure and saw this book. I have read Almond's earlier book Candyfreak and really liked it. I read another one of his books and did not care for it as much. This book seems to be about how the telling of bad stories led to our political issues with the MAGA movement. I did not know what he meant by bad stories but I was intrigued enough. I went and bought it. Reading about the political problems of our days is not the most enticing; we are living through this mess, do we need to give some of our precious reading time to it. It stays on the shelf because there might be a time I want to hear what Almond said about this mishegoss.

Copra Round One by Michelle Fiffe This is a great comic collection. Michelle Fiffe self published this series where he riffed on a DC comic from the 80s, The Suicide Squad. He changed enough of the plot to not get in trouble, but it was still the Suicide Squad. His art using colored pencils is unique. His storytelling is fast and furious. I bought it at my local comic shop when I just wanted to buy something. It remained unread for a few years until the Pandemic when I had nothing to do one early morning. I took the book down and read the whole thing. The packaging of the book is beautiful, from the French flaps to the feel of the paper used. It was great. But yet, I didn't continue reading the series. Why? Maybe because I am mostly done with superhero comics. Just because I love comics does not mean I am beholden to superheroes. It is great, but my love lies elsewhere. The final question for this book, why have I kept it? Shouldn't I give it away to someone who will love it more than I?

The Collected Works Volume 2: Munro by Jules Feiffer. In high school, we did a production of Feiffer's People and I fell in love with his work. The play consisted of performances of his comic strip from the Village Voice. I then found out that he helped write The Spirit by Will Eisner in the late 40s and was completely smitten. A while back, Fantagraphics started to do the collected works. They never finished. I think I have most of what they put out. The volumes are scattered around the various bookcases in the house. I am not sure why this one is in this bookcase. I am pretty sure I have had this for twenty years and have read it. I don't mind having it around, but I am just puzzled why it is here by the bed. I like some of the work here, but it's not my favorite. It does include Munro, which is about the little boy who is accidentally drafted into the army. It's pretty good but it is definitely of its time. This one is not going anywhere. There is no chance that I will get rid of any of my Feiffer books. The man just works for me.

The Star Diaries by Stanislaw Lem. I have been intimidated by Lem all my life as a science fiction reader. He has serious looking covers on his books and the sentences seem to go on forever. I read Solaris for a class in college and didn't like it. I don't know if that is because of the book or that it was an assignment. Now, during the first few months of the Pandemic, I discovered I missed seeing live art. I really wanted to see theater. I found this guy online who was doing one person theater in his closet, which he turned into a studio/stage. Every week he puts on a new work. A lot of it took advantage of camera tricks and pre-recorded scenes. If you timed it right, you could watch him perform it live. I saw the "live" performance of the 77th Voyage of Egon Tichy, based on a Lem story. It is about a solitary space man who flies through a part of space that causes time anomalies and he interacts with himself from the past and from the future. I don't know how they created it with him interacting with pre recorded versions of himself but it was so cool. I loved it. I watched it several times. Later that year I was trying to write in a hotel room in Northampton, Ma because Vermont was closed to out of state visitors. I was not doing great with writing, so I walked to a great used bookstore named Grey Matter books. They have the first floor of an old mill and it is teaming with many books. I saw this and found out the story they based the play on was in it. The price was 4.50. Instead of writing that evening, I read the story. It was good. I liked it. I loved the play. Is that wrong? Am I not supposed to love the adaptation? Should I always say that classic old saw, "The book was better?" But the story didn't have the virtuosity of the play version. I tried a few of the other stories and I just could not get into it. Maybe Lem and me are not meant to be best friends. Maybe I am not going to keep this book. There are people who love Lem. Why shouldn't they have this book?

Born to Be Posthumous: The Eccentric Life and Mysterious Genius of Edward Gorey by Mark Dery. I love Edward Gorey, so it is amazing that I have not read thai book. I know I spent a long evening dipping into this part and that. I will read it. But probably not the whole thing. I usually skip the first fifty pages of biographies. I don't care about the person's childhood. I just can't care less. I discovered I will not get through bios if I start with the kid stuff. I bog down in their high school years. I am reading about an artist and writer I love, I want to read about the time he wrote and drew.

State of the Union: Notes on an Obama Administration by Howard Zinn. I used to live in Waltham, so I love when I get a chance to go to Moody Street and check out the shops. I went into a bookstore that was new to me, Back Pages Books. They had nice books. The place was pleasant. I enjoyed my time there. I went to pay for the book I found for my wife (a collection of Gabriel Bell diary comics) and began to talk to the co-owner behind the counter. He was so cool. It turned out they published their own books. He was, at the moment, going through a hand written journal he found by a 19th century sailor. He was painstakingly deciphering the man's bad cursive and typing it up. He hoped that it would be published late in the year. He told me that they were getting good writers to talk to at the shop. They even got Howard Zinn to talk about Obama becoming president. They had to get a bigger space for the speech. He said Zinn was amazing and they even took the speech and made a small book. He went into a back area and came back with a copy of the book they published. Though I didn't really want the book, I was compelled to buy it. I read it and it was good. It would have been better to hear Zinn himself, but this was a good consolation prize. Of course Back Pages closed a year or so later. That breaks my heart. I want all of these bookstores and publishers to succeed. Because I want more books like this out there. I probably should give this away, but I am also happy to have it in the bookshelf. To remind me of an afternoon in Waltham where I met a guy transcribing a 150 year old journal and proudly showing off what he was making. All of these necessary things.

The Little Man: Short Stories 1980-1995 by Chester Brown. A collection of Brown's very idiosyncratic comic stories. I got this because I saw a youtube video going over two stories from this. One was about a really unpleasant neighbor. It was an autobiography. Then the next one was about creating that story. Some of the people included didn't like how they were being represented and it also showed Brown's unique style of creating a comic story. I was so intrigued so I ordered a used copy of the book online and read those two stories as soon as it came. They are fascinating. Reading a comic story about how he created the previous comic story was wild and really instructive. The other stories? I have read some of them. They are not as engaging as those two. I keep the book around because I know I will get it in my head one day that I should just knock this one out. I will not let this book go though, those two stories are really instructive on how to create and especially how to create something based on real people.

The Cruising Diaries by Brontez Purnell. I picked this up in a comic shop in Easthampton, Ma. They had a good deal of books by a publisher named Silver Sprockets. They have been putting out interesting work and this was not even a comic. It is an illustrated memoir. It is about cruising San Francisco for anonymous gay sex. This is not my life but it is a life I know so little about, so I picked it up. It certainly is a world I didn't know. The stories were detailed and kind of gross. There was some humor and some danger. The illustrations left little to the imagination. They were cartoons having sex in dirty bathrooms. I enjoyed the book, but don't feel the desire to keep it. But where do I donate it? Can't put it in the little lending libraries. Can't just donate it to Savers. I also don't want to put this in the garbage. This is a good book. But it is pretty naughty with dirty pictures. Where is the right place for this book? Until I have an answer, it stays here on the shelf.

A Collection of Sand by Italo Calvino. This is a good time for lovers of Calvino. Over the past ten years, new translations of the books that were here have come out and other volumes that never made it into English have arrived. This is one of them. I have had this for almost ten years. It is a collection of his art reviews and other essays. I have read some of it, but it is kind of dense. But I will always pick up a Calvino book I do not have. He is one of the greats. He is one of the people that changed my way of thinking. Of course I will have all his books, whether I read them or not.

This is Not a T-Shirt by Bobby Hundred. My wife got me this for Christmas. She always gifts me with books. I am not complaining. I do not know why she decided I wanted this one. It doesn't matter, it is about starting a streetwear brand. It is interesting. I just don't know why this book made her think that this would be the gift. I suppose I will only discover the answer by reading it. I could ask her, but where is the fun in that?

Why People Believe Weird Things by Michael Shermer. Two years ago, I got into a discussion/disagreement with someone at work about some weird belief they had. They were so sure they were right and I just could not figure out they believed what they believed. Why do people think stupid things? For an answer, I went online and found this book and I bought it and came and then I couldn't remember why it was so important to me learn why people believe in UFOs, Jewish Space Lasers, that the Holocaust did not happen and other things that reasonably smart people hole as truth. Why did I want to learn this? I guess when I finally remember why I needed to get this book, then I will take it off the shelf and read it and learn things I couldn't remember why I wanted to know.

My Old Nook. When I got the bookcase, I stocked it with the books around my side of the bed. There was plenty there. One of the things that was there was my old Nook ereader. I used it exclusively for four or five years. Over its life, I downloaded a ton of books on it. I don't know how many, perhaps four hundred titles. I only read a fraction of them. I used it like I used this bookshelf, a place to hold all the books I have not gotten to. The Nook is better in that it doesn't take up too much space. The nook is worse than the real bookshelf because I don't own the books on it. I just leased it. The owners of the book can decide to rescind me having it and the next time I use it, certain books will be gone. Another reason it is not as good as a regular bookshelf is that I can't find the power chord to it. It has not been used for eight years or so and I cannot access anything. If you can't read the books, then what is it: is it an ereader, a bookshelf or just something that takes up space? The final question I will ask is, why the hell did I put it on the bookshelf? What was the purpose of having this old technology mingling with books? I could read the books if I wanted. This is more a mocking thing that cannot be used, cannot be accessed. But for several years, it went wherever I went. I read it all the time. I enjoyed the weight of it. And that's all that's left. It's weight. A paperweight, if anyone ever uses those things anymore.

Bird in a Cage by Frederic Dard. This is another Dard book that I have tried several times and have not gotten into. I had another book that I couldn't get into. So what should I do? Buy another book by him. Maybe I will like it better. I don't know why I thought that. But I saw this at that wonderful Brattleboro bookshop, Mystery on Main, and convinced myself that another title by him will make me realize that I should own it and read it and love it. That did not happen. One nice thing is that I haven't bought a third book by him that I will no doubt not read as well.

BDQ: Essays and Interviews on Quebec Comics edited by Andy Brown. I never asked for this book. I never got it from a loved one. It showed up in the mail, and like that, I now own it. I heard of an art book that looked amazing from a Canadian publisher and I ordered it. It came a week later and the book is overwhelmingly wild. But the package did not just come with that book. This book was with it. It was given to me as a freebie. I didn't just get the book I ordered. I got more more more. I love books about the history of comics, so I was kind of psyched by this. But the type is small and I only have heard of one of the comic makers profiled. I write about comics for my zine, Comic Book Hinterland, so having reference materials on comics is a good thing. And I am happy to get a copy of a book that they were probably desperate to get out of their storeroom.

Three Legends: The Snow Goose, The Small Miracle, Ludmila by Paul Gallico. I had a flash fiction story published online at Every Day Fiction and the comments were positive. Two of them said that my work was very reminiscent of Paul Gallico. I never heard of him. I figured I should discover who's style I am cribbing accidentally. I happened to be in a pretty big library that day, so I found a book of Gallico and read some of it. It was about a mouse or something. It didn't do anything for me. A few years later, I was at the used bookstore I picked up The Portable Henry Rollins in and saw this book. I bought it for eight dollars. The woman who owned the shop was impressed I was getting this. She said that Gallico was a great writer and it was a shame that no one was reading him anymore. I said, "Well, I do." That wasn't true. I tried to read each of the stories in this book. They just didn't keep my interest. Maybe next time I will get through it and realize that he and I write exactly alike. Or better yet, that we are two different types of writers and that's good too.

Just the Facts: A decade of Comics Essays by David Collier. The Comic Shop near Rhode Island was too crowded. It was hard to get through the aisles. There were too many books for the small space. I was getting anxious. I never want to leave a comic shop without something, but the place was making my blood pressure rise. I found this in a section that shouldn't have had non fiction comic books. But there it was. I like comic book essays and non fiction. I think it is a great use of the medium. I never heard of Collier, but it looked good. He sold it to me for three dollars. It was a good deal. But the lettering is so small and cramped. My eyes can't do it. Though I love comics, there are just some that my eyes won't let me understand anymore. I will stell get them, because I want to be in denial of my bad eyesight. And who knows, maybe my doctor will finally get me the miracle glasses that will allow me to read comics like I did when I was a kid.

Sonnets by Jorge Luis Borges. When my wife sees any new Borges in English she buys it for me. I so appreciate that because reading his piece, Borges and I changed the way I thought of literature as well as expanded what I think of the inner self. That little piece of writing is such a powderkeg and I will always love Borges. I have a good amount of his work in English. This book took all of the Sonnets he wrote, in a variety of books, and put them together. Why have I not read it? Because sonnets are hard for me to focus on. I love poetry but reading through a poetry book is something I don't have a talent for. Only this week, knowing that I was to write about it for this biography of a bookshelf, did I realize that I was doing it all wrong. I should just have this on my bedside and read one or two of the sonnets before going to bed. It will take only a few minutes and in a few months, I will have gotten through another book by Borges. I am excited by this obvious plan, because Borges always challenges and surprises me. Let's see if this works.

Watchfires by Hilary Plum. I bought this when we went to a nice bookstore in Rhode Island called the Savoy. Despite there being a lot of cool things, I hail maryed this book. I didn't know what else to get. This has a book black and red cover. It is square shaped. It feels good in the hand. The type is large and readable to me.The back cover blurbs promise a new form of non-fiction. I am sold. Haven't tried to read it. Its been with me for five years, and yet, it remains unread. I don't know why. Sometimes, books just want to be left alone. Sometimes they are not ready to be opened and devoured. They enjoy their quiet monk's life on the shelf. Who am I to deny them such splendid isolation?

Bandit Love by Massimo Carlotto. Bandit Love is such a cool title. Everyone should have a book called Bandit Love on their bookshelf. We got this at an amazing bookstore in the North End of Boston. My wife discovered it and could not wait for me to check it out. It is IAM Books. IAM stands for Italian American. And that is a perfect way to describe this shop. It had books by Italian writers and books about Italy. Some of the books were in Italian, but a good deal of them were in English. I was really loving what I was seeing and would have wanted to spend more time deciding what to buy there, but that's when the tour group came in. It seems that this woman is a tour guide for the North End and one of the stops of the tour is this bookshop. It must be good for business, but it was running us out. There were now twenty new people in the bookshop blocking the aisles listening to the tour guide go on and on. My wife and son were looking frustrated with this as well. I went to the mystery section, saw this title and got my way to the cashier. It was a hasty purchase, but I think it is a good one. I have not gotten to it for no other reason than that there are so many books ahead of it. There is something about the way the book feels that you know it's going to be a good one.

The Road Home by Ai Wei. This was another hail mary purchase. I was at a good bookstore and could not find anything and then I saw this. This is a Penguin Specials where I guess the covers mimic the covers Penguin used to produce in the 40s. The bland cover that does not try to sell you to buy this book. This is the world's most boring cover and I wanted to read the book that earned such a cover. It didn't hurt that the book was a short one. If you are trying out a new author, you should start with the short book because if you don't dig the writer, you haven't invested too much time into them. But is it true that I will read this book primarily because it has a super boring cover? Yeah. That kind of thing gets me through the door. Sign me up for the blandest of covers.

The Haggis by Clarissa Dickson Wright. No. This is not a mystery novel, but it should be. The Haggis seems perfect for a locked room whodunnit. No. This is a guide to the history and use of the haggis. I like haggis. It's the scotts in me, but I find it delicious. I haven't had it in several years, but that taste is not something you don't forget easily. My wife got me this small little field guide to the wild and wacky world of Haggis when she was traveling in Scotland. It still has the price tag of five pound, ninety nine. Kind of pricey for such a tiny thing. To be fair, I thought it was a slightly jokey gift. But on looking at it just now, I am intrigued by what I saw in the book and now I want to read it. This is what's happening with this project. I look at a book and decide I must read it next. Of course that is a useless promise when I say it about twenty different books.

The Glob by John O'Reilly and Walt Kelly. A fun romp through the history of first man and evolution where we follow the amorphous creature called the Glob. Now I read this but I am happy to have this near me on this bookshelf because the illustrations by Walt Kelly are just absolutely delightful. I love Walt Kelly, but these illustrations seem even more inspired than what he was doing in his Pogo daily strip. My wife and I went to a bookshop in Vermont that was closing its brick and mortar shop. It was a great bookshop and it was giving pretty good discounts. Near the end of our time there, we looked at their high end books near the register and I found such things I had never seen before. I saw this and was shocked because I never knew about this book and oh how I wanted it. I don't know if it is valuable, but to me, I just knew that I needed it. WIth the discount, I paid 37 dollars for it and I have not regretted that one bit. Well. Maybe a little. But that will be continued on with the next book discussed.

Simple's Uncle Sam by Langston Hughes. In the 90s and the 2000s, there were always books you saw in used bookstores. They always popped up and I always moved right past them. One of the things I noticed were a bunch of Simple books by Langston Hughes. What were they? I only knew Hughes as a poet. What were these things? I eventually bought one for four dollars at some local used book shop. And then it stayed on a shelf for years until I started reading about Langston Hughes for a project and realized that this guy did so much more than poetry (which is pretty good by itself). The Simple stories were published weekly for years in several black newspapers. They were about a guy named Simple and the things he said and did in the bar he hung out at in Harlem. This was right up my alley. I love bar stories. I also love columns about current affairs masquerading as a short story. So I read it and I loved it. I found one of my favorite lines that Hughes wrote in this book. "It's a good thing folks cannot crack the heart and drop their insides in a frying pan like an egg. It's a good thing a man cannot make an omelet out of your trouble." I should have gotten more books about Simple. This one is great. Now, let's go back to the time I was in Vermont at a used bookstore. I had already found The Glob and was sure to take it home, but I kept on looking at the high end shop. There I saw an old paperback of Simple stories. This was the first Simple book Hughes published back in the 1940s. I had never seen it. It was pricey. With the going out of physical building business discount, it would have been over fifty dollar and I still planned on picking up The Glob. This was tough. I was talking to my wife about this. I said I see the Simple books from time to time, though I never saw this one. I probably will have a shot to pick it up somewhere down the line. The owner of the store came by and added, "I am not forcing you to buy this, but in my experience, the time to buy a book is when you see it. What are the chances you will find this again?" She made a good point and yet I still passed on it. And I never saw it again. And I don't even see the later Simple books anymore. They are getting harder to find as it is harder to find used book shops. I keep SImple's Uncle Sam around because I love it and it reminds me a truth I should have already known, "If you want a book that's in your hand, then buy that book."

Nathan Never: Bauhaus Killer. I am not sure who the writer and artist are. This is a monthly issue of a long running Italian comic series. It is a graphic novel because their monthly comics are 96 pages square bound affairs. It is in Italian so I will not be reading it any time soon. I do look at it because I enjoy the art. It feels similar to the work of Howard Chaykin. They also drew two characters to look just like John Travolto and Samuel L Jackson in their Pulp Fiction roles. I got it from the North End Italian bookshop IAM books that I got Bandit Love in. They had a section of used Italian comics and I got a few Dylan Dog volumes (can't read those either) and this one. This one was one dollar. What will I do with a book I cannot read? Do you have to be able to read the words to like the comic?

A Devil Comes to Town by Paolo Maurensig. I got this at the Bookloft in Great Barrington, Ma. I liked the look of it. It is short and that always works for me. It also seemed to have a fairy tale-like vibe and that also works for me. What doesn't work for me is the strong desire to put all other things on hold and read it right now.

The Wasteland by Martin Rowson. The large used bookshop in Hadley, Ma, Grey Matter Books, has a section in the way back filled with comic strip collections and graphic novels. THis one got my attention because I never heard of it. It was put out by Harper and Row books, so that's no joke. It was from 1990. I didn't know it existed until I had it in my hand. I kind of pride myself with knowing a lot of the graphic novels and comics from that era, but this one was a mystery. It seems to be a mashup of 40s detective fiction and T.S. Eliot's The Wasteland. This could be a very cool thing. But the art is harsh. It is good for what they were trying to do, but just not to my liking. The lettering is also a strange ornamental font and it just makes it hard for me to read it. I will try it one day. Yeah. One day.

Wax Museum Movies by George Higam. My wife was going to a small press conference and she told me that McFarland has great books. I looked it up online and said if they had the book about Wax Museum Movies, I would love to get it. They had sold out when she got to their table, but they backordered it for her. It took months but when it came, I was so happy. Why did I want it so? Because the idea of a comprehensive book about all the movies that feature wax museums is the craziest, most delightful thing I have heard. The book is written by someone who has created wax figures and works for the New York City morgue. If we can have an expert on these movies, it probably is this guy. The book is a reference. They don't make easy bedtime reading. But every time I encounter a movie with a wax museum (and based on the weird movies I watch, it happens frequently enough) I will reach for this book and read his opinion on the Wax Museum I just saw. When I was writing my book on the Inner Sanctum movies, I entertained myself with the entry on the Frozen Ghost film. I almost want to watch more wax mausoleum movies just for more of an excuse to read the entries. But I have seen enough wax museum movies to know that that might be a dangerous path.

Disfigured: On Fairy Tales, Disability and Making Space by Amanda Leduc. I don't remember when and where I got this book. I know that it is an interesting and unique way to look at disability. I just don't remember when I picked it up. I haven't gotten to it, but I like to have books on fairy tales around. I am fascinated by fairy tales and have used them in my writing. Up in the attic, I have two bookshelves filled with fairy tales from around the world and books discussing fairy tales from around the world. This is one that is so wild an idea that I want to have it near me. Ready to be engaged with.

The Stuffed Owl: An Anthology of Bad Verse edited by DB Wyndham Lewis and Charles Lee. We got this at a great nearby bookshop, Quabog Books. I don't know when we picked it up, but the why is obvious. It is a book teeming with bad poetry. Who doesn't want that around? I have read the occasional poem from it and that stuff is bad. And funny.

Art Wars by Francis Deschrnais. This is a translation of a French language comic book that might be one of the best things I have read in a long time. It is on this bookshelf because I am not sure what I should put the books I adore and do not ever want to part with. I really think this is great. It is about aliens coming and stealing all the Earth's artists because in space, the creation of art can be used as a weapon. It is funny and smart and it is told with limited images. This is a minimalist comic where there are only ten different images reused throughout the book. The dialogue changes but the images stay the same and yet, it is one of the most engaging graphic novels I have ever come across. I am happy this was on this bookshelf because this gives me a chance to tell everyone to find this book. You will be so happy if you do.

Titanic Tales edited by Marc Wheately. I have been a fan of Marc Wheately's comic book work since I was a kid. But I never knew of this. He put out his own pulp fiction collection of stories and comic art. The type is small and my eyes are just getting old. But I saw it at the Book Mill in Montaque last year and I knew I had to own it. It is pulp fiction, which I love. It is also by a creator I dig and never knew of this. I hope to get to it. I want to get to it. But it is a lot of pages. A lot of words. Little words. But I don't want to miss such joy, such thrills.

Troublemaker by Joseph Hansen. Wandering around Gibson's in Concord Ma, I found these reissues of Hansen's books. I didn't know of him. It is a gay private eye in the 1970s, written in the 70s. This looks really good. I will get to you. I am so interested. Well, interested enough to have you in the bookcase near the bed. That's prime territory. That's reading when I can't sleep territory. That's a good place for a book to be and I am happy you are part of the team. Now get back there on the shelf and wait like a good little piece of a little known history.

Noir by Richard Matheson. I got this for 7.50 at Gray Matter Books. I love Richard Matheson. I Am Legend is one of the great books I read when I was a teenager. And now I have a collection of three of his crime novels? So cool. I have tried to read each of the three novels in this book and haven't been able to get myself into them. I think that is my problem and not the book, so I will try again. I owe Matheson that much. He helped make me the kind of reader I am.

Envisioning Jacob's Ladder: Religion, Representation and Allusion in American Visual Culture 1750-2000 by David M. Hummon. That's a mouthful of a title. This is the only art exhibition catalog in this bookcase. I have many catalogs. When my wife and I started together, we went to a lot of museum shows and if there was a catalog for the show, I would pick it up. There is a bookcase in the attic that is laden with these catalogs. That's where this was for quite some time. The show about Jacob's Ladder was at the gallery at the College of the Holy Cross, which is close to us. The show was fascinating, telling of the history of the shape of Jacob's Ladder and its varied meanings. It was cool. But they had no catalog. Years go by and I am at the gallery again and there is a copy of the catalog. I scooped it up and read about half of the text. Reading texts in catalogs is tough, but sometimes they can give me ideas on things to write about. That's why this is down on this bookshelf. Last year, I was working on a novelette called 258 Steps to the Floor of Heaven. It was a weird piece that dealt with steps and heaven and faith and all that stuff. Near the end, I thought I might want to bring in concepts of Jacob's Ladder into the book. I brought this catalog down from the attic and put it in the case by the bed, where it would be ready to help me with the book. The thing was, I never used it. I went in a different direction with the text. So this book is ready to leave its space in the bedroom and go back to the attic. If I ever have another story where I might want to include a Jacob's Ladder metaphor, I will know where the information is. In the attic.

Things You've Always Wanted to Know About Monsters But Were Afraid to Ask by Tony Tallarico. Just like the last book, this is in this bookshelf because I was using it as reference for a writing project. That was called 100 Monsters. I got in my head the idea of a list memoir where I would go through 100 monsters I was obsessed with before I was 13.

Each chapter was a discussion of the monster and why I dug it as a kid. While I was working on it, I had a memory that I had a book as a kid that had many little articles about classic monster movies. That was this book. I figured I could use my love of that book and the monsters I discovered in its pages as part of 100 Monsters. The only problem was, I didn't have a copy of the book. Do not worry, Dave. There is such a thing as online bookstores. A used copy was mailed to me within days and I had a wonderfully nostalgic afternoon going through this old friend. I don't know how many times I read it when I was a kid, but it must have been a ton because when I was looking at again as an adult, I was able to anticipate what monster was going to be discussed on the next page.That project was completed, but I don't know if I am through with this book. I might want to read it again. Or just flip through it and remind myself of a time when loving monsters was the best thing a kid could do.

The Written World and the Unwritten World by Italo Calvino. Another Calvino essay collection that I haven't read yet. Love Calvino. This one is about writing and reading. This should be good. It's Calvino. How can it be anything other than great?

The Regulars by Sarah Stolfa. This book has been by my bedside for eleven or twelve years and I don't think it will ever part from its perch. I love this book. I might go several years without looking at it, but I will go back to it and admire it so much. It is a book of photographs of the regulars of a dive bar in Philadelphia. The photographer was a bartender there and took these beautiful full faced color photographs of the regulars at the bar. Most of them have beer and cigarettes in front of them. It is such an evocative picture of bar life. These people are sad and lonely and drunk and defiant and there is so much life in these photos. My wife got it for me after she saw me flipping through it at River Run

Books in Portsmouth, New Hampshire. I even used this book for writing prompts for myself. I had a notion of looking at each of the regulars and imagining what folk tale or creation myth they would want to tell the bartender. I wrote twelve of them but lost my focus on it. I did put out what I wrote as a chapbook called Barstool Mythologies and I still want to go back to finish it. It's the faces in the pages that haunt me, that make me want to create. I actually went to the bar where the photos were taken. Mh wife was in Philadelphia and I stumbled upon it. I was not planning on drinking at 11 in the morning, but there I was drinking. It was 2016 and for some reason, there was still smoking in the place. Every space at the bar had an ashtray. I loved being there, but it is odd that I fanboyed at a dive bar in a different state. But there I was. Let's hear it for a great photo book. It did not stay away from me.

The Collected Plays Volume 4 by Harold Pinter. A friend told me she was seeing a revival of Betrayal on Broadway. I was jealous. I wanted to see that play. I wanted to see serious drama on Broadway. Instead I was at Bedlam Books and I saw this book. It had Betrayal in it. This seemed too much a coincidence to be anything but fate. I bought it, but I wasn't able to read the play. I used to read plays all the time. I have a full bookcase in the attic of collected plays. But I have fallen out of the habit of reading plays. It's not the easiest thing to do because plays are written to be performed and not to be read in bed on a lazy Saturday morning. I tried later that day to read it and it just wasn't happening. So I went on line and found a recording of a performance of the play for the BBC. I followed along in the book. I thought the play was good, but not brilliant. I had heard of this play for years and I was expecting it to be the best thing ever. My friend came back from Broadway and told me the same thing, the acting was awesome and the play was, well, it was fine. There are other plays in the book. Do I have the strength to try to read them too?

Pasha the Persian by Margaret Linden with Illustrations by Milt Gross. I bought this at Gray Matter books because I saw the name Milt Gross. I love Milt Gross. He was a cartoonist in the first half of the 20th century. His stuff is big and funny as hell. He drew comic strips, wrote books in a thick Yiddish dialect, wrote scenarios for Charlie Chaplin movies and drew comic books. He even wrote what is considered to be one of the first graphic novels, He Done Her Wrong. Check him out, he is a hell of a good time. Cartoonists made money illustrating humorous books and this was one of them. I bought it for five dollars. I could have just looked at the illustrations and been happy. And that's mostly what I have done with it. But with me focusing on these books on this bookshelf, I started reading the book. Margaret Linden was a Broadway actress. She wrote this book about her own cat. She even put herself into the book. I don't know if I am really loving the story, but I get excited when I flip a page and another Milt Gross drawing shows up. When I am done with it, will it stay in this bookcase? I don't think so. I think I will put this up to the bookcase in the attic that has a bunch of my comic related books, including other books by Milt Gross.

The Wise Men of Helm and Their Meffy Tales by Solomon Simon. A collection of the shtetl folk tales with a font that even I can read it? Of course I want to read this book. But I don't. Too painful. This was given to me by my dear friend Richard Fox the last time I saw him. He was home after a stay in hospice care. His little dog stayed guard on his lap. He talked to us for two hours before he was too fatigued to go on. He spoke of poetry and going to school in St Louis. He spoke of friends and he sang praises on the poets we have in Worcester. He was so kind and generous. He looked at the coffee table and saw this book. "You should have this Dave. This is right up your alley." Of course he was right. He died a few months later. I want to read this book. Richard gave it to me not to just keep it on a bookshelf. He wanted me to love something that he loved. There is so much emotion and personal affection embedded in this book that I have not read.

The Damned and the Beautiful: American Youth in the 1920s by Paula S Pass. And now. A mystery. Why the hell do I have this book? I have no memory of this book. It is something I am interested in, though it is a thick book and I don't usually go for long books. I asked my wife if she gave it to me. She looked at it like she had never seen it before, because she hadn't. "Did some other woman give this to you?" she asked. I rolled my eyes. Yeah, pretty women want to give me books I probably will never get around to reading. That happens all the time. But we still have the issue. Where is this book from and should I let it go? If I do, maybe someone who really wants it will find it. Maybe I am the unhappy sojourn that never ends and it needs to continue on with it's journey. Or to be more honest, I can put it in a free library and have a little more space in the shelf.

The Shelf on the Top of the Case That Is No Good for Books

It's not really a shelf. It is just at the top of the bookshelf. There are no sides so it won't be good for books. But that does not stop me from using it for comic books. I have two piles of comics piled up about two feet. There are a lot of comics there. The funny thing is, these are new comics from the last four years. I didn't own any of these comics before the pandemic.

With the pandemic I had a lot of time to watch videos online and one thing was comics. There were a lot of videos about finding wonders in dollar and fifty cent bins. And when I was able to go out and go to comic shops, I hit the dollar bins. A thing I rarely did.

I picked up weird things I thought I would like. I got a bunch of Roarin' Rick's Rarebit Fiends comics which are Rick Veitch's dream comics. I was picking up anthology comics. I was picking up comics with art by Kirby or Ditko that made it to the bargain bin.

I read some. I didn't read others. But there are now hundreds of these things. Where the hell will they go? I actually picked up comic boxes and filled four of them with these dollar bin purchases. These two piles are the ones that still just are hanging around. It is a physical representation of the boredom and the varied interests of pandemic time. Some people learned how to make sourdough bread. Mr? I was able to get the entire 19 issues of the Human Fly comic book all from the dollar bins. Such a joy.

I will not go through them one by one as I do the books. The books are the real thing for a bookshelf. The comics are merely squatters. They are just there until the government check comes in so they can get a better place to hang out.

It has gotten harder to read comics, just as comics are more difficult with my aging eyes. One more reminder of me getting old. Can't even read a comic easily. Ah well. At least I can still look at the pictures.

The Bottom Shelf (Which is Bigger than the others and can take larger books)

Going Left to Right

Enchanted: A History of Fantasy Illustration edited by Jesse Kowalski. This is a very thorough exhibition catalog for a show at the Norman Rockwell Museum a few years ago. This is a lovely thing with a ton of scholarly essays I will probably not even attempt to read. We were staying nearby in West Stockbridge, so I took George, my son with me. He was not enthusiastic. He informed us that he doesn't like modern art or museums. My wife and I met at a museum. We love art and going to see it. George went to his first museum when he was seven weeks old. He cried throughout that Andy Warhol exhibit. I am sure he was not the only one. We took him to the museum all the time growing up. But as a teenager he found the voice to tell us he doesn't dig it. But I wanted to see this art show and I was taking him. He told me later that this was one of the only art shows he liked. It was fantasy paintings. They were cool. That made the afternoon a rousing success. Of course I would get the catalog to celebrate Geore not hating going to a museum.

The Apex Treasury of Underground Comics Edited by Don Donahue and Susan Goodrick. This was published in 1974. It is an excellent collection of the best of the underground comics scene. It is the first book that the original Maus story by Art Spiegelman appeared in. It was first in a comic Funny Aminals two years before, but now it is in a real book. I have always wanted a copy of Funny Aminals because Maus is so important to me. This is a good consolation prize. This book is another instance of buy the book you dig when you see it. I saw it at a wonderful West Stockbridge bookstore, but I just couldn't justify the

35 dollars for it. But I kept on thinking about it. I kept on wondering why I didn't just get it. We came back to the bed and breakfast near the bookstore six months later and I was there as soon the shop opened. There it was. I didn't lose my chance for it. I went and bought it without even looking at it. It was only when we are back at the b&b that I looked at the book and realized that the cover is a Crumb illustration of a gutter with a large turd sitting on a discarded underground comic. The cover is gross. I kind of hate it. I must admit, I might not have read anything in this book because I hate the cover to much. It doesn't stop the fact that this is a great volume of important underground comic strips. But why does it have to have shit on the cover?

Forever and a Death by Donald E. Westlake. Let us now praise spouses or partners who know what books you want to read. I am so blessed. She knows the books that I will dig. With this one, it was easy. I adore Westlake. I must have read thirty of his books, and there are still more to read, which is wonderful. It is also put out by Hard Case Crime that makes a great package from cover to formatting. This one is long and that's why I probably haven't tackled it yet. I like books to be 200 pages or less. That's not a hard rule, but I tend to pick up thinner books. But this looks pretty awesome. The introduction talks about how this was originally a pitch for a James Bond movie. It was rejected, so Westlake changed enough of it and made it his own James Bond like book. Part of me wants to read everything from a favorite writer right away, but that would mean there is nothing else to read. Maybe it's best to take my time reading his work. How's that for an excuse?

Killer, Come Back to Me: The Crime Stories of Ray Bradbury. Another Hard Case Crime book my wife got me. Another excellent choice. Haven't read it. I have not enjoyed the last few Bradbury books I have tried. I think its me that changed. I think he was perfect when I was 14 years old. Now that I am 54, his little linguistic tricks don't go far with me. But this is a collection of crime stories that has got to be good. I will get to it. I just don't want to be disappointed. I want to love Bradbury again like I did when I was a kid.

I Used to Be Charming: The Rest of Eve Babitz. I only discovered Babitz five years ago. It has been love ever since. She, to my mind, is the great writer of 1970s Los Angeles. She was just so good. My wife got this for me for Christmas. I have read some of the articles in the book. But I am taking my time. She passed away a few years ago, and so there will be no more work by her. Once I finish this, that's it. No more Babitz. Sometimes it is wise to dawdle while finishing a book. Especially if it is a book that prides itself with being "the rest."

Dust & Grooves: Adventures in Record Collecting by Eilon Paz. I love this book. I hate this book. This book is great. This book is a pain. Let me put it plainly. This is a coffee table. What is a coffee table book? It is a book so damned oversized that the coffee table is the only place where you can keep it. Or you can have it sideways in a bottom shelf of a bookcase like this one. How do you read a book this heavy? This large? How do you cozy up to it? No. Really. I would like to know. I don't read books on lecterns. I don't own a lectern (though that would be pretty neat to have, wait, no, no lectern!) I hold a book in front of my eyes and read it. This would be like doing a deadlift. Books that are good for your muscle toning. I just weighed the book and it is five pounds. Doesn't sound like much? Then you hold it while reading it for a half hour and tell me if this is a breezy reading experience. I guess I am a little flummoxed because this book is awesome. Given to me as a gift, I adore it. It is filled with beautiful color photographs of record collections and record stores. I love LPs and this is perfect for me. But the book is also chock-a-block with essays and interviews. And then I ask, how the hell do I read this? I mean, I want to. I can go on looking at the pictures, but I feel like I am missing out all the book has to offer. By the way, the book has a great photo of one of my favorite Massachusetts record stores, Mystery Train in Amherst. Love that place. How can I not love this book? A book I don't know how to read.

Disorderly Elements by Bob Cook. Oh. You can judge a book by its cover. I saw this at one of the closing days of Mystery on Main in Brattleboro (right before the owner retired) and loved the cover photograph. It is a black and white photo of a man in a bowler hat and top coat up to the waste in the ocean. He holds a black leather briefcase over his head. The photo is awesome and I had to buy the book. I knew I would love any story that attached itself to that image. The font of the text is readable and the books is designed to be held and read. The back has a little blurb that reads, "Who's Like to Like This? Fans of Ross Thomas." Two things with that. First, what a smart way to get someone to buy the book by putting similar writers on the back cover. And second, I like Ross Thomas. I hope the blurb and the cover photograph aren't lying to me and I will like the story.

Marvel Preview #17: Blackmark by Gil Kane. This is a magazine, but a full graphic novel is in it and I know I want this nearby when I want some science fantasy adventure with great Gil Kane art. In the early 1970s, Kane wanted to get into book publishing and put out with Bantam books, the paperback called Blackmark. I have a copy of it and I love it. The story is lame but the art is fantastic. I only found out much later that Kane could not get the second volume published, due to the first one not doing well. What to do with a full second volume? You

have your friends at Marvel Comics Magazine department to put it out.
I picked it up right before pandemic lockdown thinking I would read it
right away. The problem is, the story is just not that great. It is written
more like an illustrated novel, which is not the easiest way to get into it.
But I will. I owe it to Gil Kane, a comic maker I have always adored.

The Comics Journal LIbrary Volume 9: Zap: The Interviews. I love
the history of comics more than I like the comics themselves in some
circumstances. I love how this wonderfully anarchic medium was
created. Underground comix can be tough for me to love, but I adore
hearing how they put out the comics they wanted and didn't care what
the mainstream wanted. I got this at the bookshop in West Stockbridge.
This was a volume that went with Fantagraphics putting out the
collected Zap Comix. These are interviews with Crumb, Shelton, Spain,
Griffin and all the rest. I have read some of it and think its great. I write
about comics for a zine I put out, having these types of resources are
so important. And it is a nice thing to flip though. You can't deny the
importance of that.

Penny Dreadfuls compiled by Stefan Dziemianowicz. This is one of
those cheap Barnes and Noble collections they would sell in the front
of the store. This was eight dollars. I love Penny Dreadfuls and Dime
Novels. I own a few examples. I love the idea of cheap sensational
magazines as the working class literature. I have always dug it. This book
is puzzling though. It has a lot of nice work in it, but most of them
were not published in the penny dreadfuls. The book has the entire
manuscript of Jekyll and Hyde and I love it, but that ain't a penny
dreadful story. Neither is the work of Arthur Conan Doyle and
Maupassant. They have similarities and I like having these stories, but it
feels like false advertising. The book does have parts of String of Pearls,

which is a Sweeny Todd penny dreadful. That's the real thing, but the others are just freaky stories published on better paper. I am not against this book. I am just against its title.

Rotten Movies We Love: Cult Classics, Underrated Gems, and Films So Bad They're Good by Rotten Tomatoes. Someone gave this to me as a present for the holidays for my birthday or because I am awesome and deserved a present. I love stuff like this. It is a fun one to dip into. They have some movies that are great and some I will never see again. But it's a fun way to be reminded that movies don't have to be serious. Sometimes you want a movie like Teen Wolf and Event Horizon.

Crap: A History of Cheap Stuff in America by Wendy A. Woloson. I picked this up at Bedlam Books in Worcester because I thought it would help me come up with ideas for my monthly column in the Worcester Review. I write a thing called The Library of Disposable Art where I talk about the stuff we love and refuse to get rid of (like all these books). I have been doing it for four years and coming up with ideas can be hard at this point. So this book seemed like a good way to get my ideas flowing. It's been a year since I bought this book and I have not once used it to help me find column ideas. I guess when I do read it, it will just be for fun.

Gone With the Ape by Dale Anglund and Janis Hirsch. This is a book that. Sometimes you just want to read a. The reason this book is awesome is because. Yeah. I have no idea what the hell this book is. I bought it in West Stockbridge because I knew this would never show up again. It was made in the 70s during the ape and gorilla trend going around. Were gorilla's big in the 70s? I have no idea. It is a scrapbook type book where we are showed the importance of apes in history and pop culture. There are many pictures of people in gorilla suits. It is all a lot of silliness and I want to spend a boring afternoon reading it. Its just that when I have a boring afternoon, I forget to look for this book.

New Jersey as Non-Site. Someone gave this to me. I said thanks. I didn't ask what the hell it was. But I don't know what it is. It has been hanging around for several years being resoundingly unclassifiable. It is an art catalog. I think. This is what the back of the book says, "New Jersey became one of the principal laboratories for experimental art after the Second World War. Between 1950 and 1975, a host of innovative artists flocked to the state's most desolate peripheries. There, in its industrial wastescapes, crumbling cities, pastoral ruins, crowded highways and banal suburbs, they produced some of the most important work of their careers." Okay. I guess it could be interesting. But I am plagued with why I have this and why someone thought that this was the book for me. I am not saying that it isn't the book for me, just wondering why others thought that.

Norwegian Folktales of Asbjjornsen & Moe. I like folktale collections. There is that. My wife got this for me at the Clark Institute of Art. We saw a show of a Norwegian artist who used aspects of folklore in their work. The gift shop included this book and Heather got it for me. Cool. She knows that when I look at a folklore infused painting I will want a book about that folklore.

Yiddish Proverbs edited by Hana J Ayalth. It is just what it seems to be. A collection of yiddish sayings. I got it at a large Plainville Massachusetts bookstore that is no longer there. It was part of a box set of Jewish writing. I love this book and will dip into it frequently. I love these expressions. My favorite is, "If God lived on Earth, people would break his windows."

The Anatomy of Story by John Truby. Another book on how to be a good writer. I figure if I read enough of them, I won't suck as much as I do. I know nothing about this book. I don't know who gave it to me. I have not read a word. But I am not going to get rid of it. It might be the answer. It might be the secret password to being a great writer. The chances are slim, but I ain't going to give up on any book that might have truth I have not considered.

The Faith of a Writer by Joyce Carol Oates. She's a good writer. She's a good teacher. It ain't a bad book to have lurking about.

Votes for Women: The Battle for the 19th Amendment: A Comics Anthology edited by Ally Shwed. Through a kickstarted campaign, I got a small comic called Bear Plane by Ally Shwed and I adored it. My wife saw it and loved it too. My son, ten years old at the time, read it and laughed out loud. With that recommendation, I will always buy her work. This was a kickstarter she put together for the 100th anniversary of the 19th amendment. I supported it and was happy to get the book. All the work is created by female identifying cartoonists. At 200 pages, it is a little daunting. I am looking forward to going through it, whenever that will be.

Prez by Joe Simon and Jerry Grandenetti. A collection of all the Prez comics. There were not a lot of them, thank goodness. This is one of the stranger DC comics from the 1970s. It was about a teenager who became president. It is seriously weird. I got it in the comics section of Ollie's for three dollars. After reading two issues, I was in love with the comic. But I read the third issue in the book and it exhausted me. I put the book down for a few days until I was ready to deal with all the weirdness. That was two years ago.

Paperback Crush by Gabrielle Moss. Heather got this for me and I can't figure out why I haven't read this. This is a book made for me. A frothy look at the YA literature of the 80s and 90s. I think it must have gotten put in this bottom shelf and then forgotten about. It is kind of hard to see what is on the bottom shelf. So we have the Babysitters Club and Sweet Valley High and onto Flowers in the Attic. There are too many cool books. And many of them are in this bookcase.

The Postman Always Rings Twice, Double Indemnity, Mildred Pierce and Selected Stories by James M Cain. Heather and I got this at a large used book store in Santa Rosa, California during our honeymoon. According to the flap, it cost us 13 dollars, which seems a lot for a used book in 2005, but it was our honeymoon and I guess we were being expansive with our shopping. I have read Postman from this book and half of Double Indemnity. I know I should get it back. Heather read a good deal of the work in the book. It is nice that we still have this. It is nice that there is still more to read in it. Better than just a thing we read back then that is taking up space.

The Incredible Hulk: From the Marvel UK Vaults. This is a cool buy from Ollies for four dollars. It is a collection of the Hulk stories from the 70s and 80s made exclusively for the British market. There are a lot of adventures and a good deal of prose stories. I find it interesting to see a British view of an American product. The comics were originally published in magazines that were larger than this so the comics are pretty cramped, making it not the most fun thing to read. But I love having it.

The Girl's Number Doesn't Answer by Talmage Powell. Picked up at the Brattleboro shop, Mystery on Main. That was one of the best bookstores I have ever been too. I only went there for two years before it closed and I have so many books from there. I am lucky that I stumbled into it. I am lucky that there were such stores. I hope that such stores still exist. I got this for the title. It is one of the great Noir titles. It is so much fun. It's a reprint of an ole 50s paperback original. I think I read half of it and didn't continue because when I picked it up, I had not a single memory of what was going on in the story. Maybe that's me. Maybe this deserves a second try. I mean, it does have a great title. That should count for something.

Nelvana of the Northern Lights by Adrian Dingle. The amazing adventures of a snow goddess who is one of the few Canadian superheroes. This collects all of the Nelvana stories from the 1940s. Canada needed to make their own superheroes during World War Two because they couldn't get American imports at the time. So they created Nelvana and others. I picked this up and think its neat, but the storytelling from Golden Age comics can be rushed and repetitive, so I kind of stalled out a third of the way through. I probably will want to get back to it. One of the most interesting things about this particular book is that the last page states that it was printed on demand On August 14th, 2020. That was the day after I ordered it. It got to me on the 16th. What a strange and wonderful world where you can own a specific copy of a book that did not exist three days prior. Does it make books more important or more disposable?

Writers Under Surveillance: The FBI Files edited by JPat Brown, BCD Lipton and Michael Morisy. One of the coolest places I ever took my son was the Spy Museum in Washington DC. He loved it. Hell, I loved it. It was smart and informative and a lot of fun. One of the best parts was the expansive gift shop. George got t-shirts and some books and I found this book. It is FBI files of them going after certain writers. It is not a reading friendly book, but it is so damned cool. I mean, James Baldwin and Gore Vidal are a focus of the FBA and here are the files to prove it. I don't know why it was so important for me to have this book, but I had to have it. It is just one of those crazy books that seem like a good idea when you buy. And it stays a good idea.

World Within A Song by Jeff Tweedy. I like his band Wilco. I have a couple of his other books. He is a decent writer. I got it this Christmas. I read half of it when I couldn't sleep because I was ravaged by flu. I don't think people should read books when they are sick as hell. It makes me have a weird feeling of relapse when I pick the book up again. It reminds me I was sick and desperate to distract my brain. But I do want to read it. He goes through a variety of songs he heard and how they affected his life. This is a perfect kind of book by a guy who thinks about songs all the time. Yes. I will read it. Don't ask me when. Just take it as faith that I will. And when I do read it, where will it go? Will it stay in this bookcase or be shipped off to the attic or will I donate it to a little library. It is hard to say. But not to worry. The important part is that it will be read.

Step Away from the Bookcase

And those are the books on the shelf. It took 19 days to write this book. It 's a book, right? Sure. It's a book .And in those 19 days, the books I focused on were affected. Anything that is observed will change. And these books were observed.

I listened to an audiobook of the Heinlein book so I could return the paperback copy to my friend Bob. I moved the Oz books to the attic and put some other books that were piled on the floor in their space. With the Borges Sonnets book, I am reading two or three sonnets a day. They are lovely and I am happy to be getting to them. At this rate, I will be done with that book in two months. But that's okay, it will get done.

I have reminded myself of certain books that I should get to next. I was really loving the Jeff Tweedy book and I have to get back to it soon. I should try the Calvino book about writing soon as well. But I know myself, and I will be distracted by the newest thing I buy or some book I am told about by a friend. I lose myself to the new and the shiny.

This project makes me realize how important a good bookstore is. Sure, I bought books online. But it is being in a bookstore that is so necessary. This is a love letter to Gibson's, R.J. Julia, That's Entertainment, The Book Loft, Shaker Mill Books, Bedlam Books, Tidewater Books, Quabog Books and all the others I brazenly neglected to mention. They give me joy just thinking of them.

If you decide to try this, writing a biography of one of your bookcases, I would love to read it. Maybe your book will find its way on my bookshelf. We should be so lucky.

David

April 18, 2924

About the Book

Bookcases lie in wait.

They are teeming with books. Some of them you have read. Some of them you were given as gifts. Other books were bought with enthusiasm and then ignored. Forgotten.

Bookcases tell the story of a the owner of the books. They tell you what his interests are and where he buys his books. What stores does he loiter in?

This is a memoir of five years of buying and reading and not reading books. David goes through each of the books in the bookcase and tells the story of why he has the book and why he hasn't read it.

It tells you the life of someone who loves and believes in books. You should get this and put this on your bookshelf. Go ahead and complete the circle.

About the Writer

Dave likes books. You have just read about a couple hundred of them. Dave also likes writing. You can see that as well, though you might not like how he writes. You cannot deny that he enjoys doing it. There are a few similar memoirs he has created. There is Century Bookshelf that talks about a hundred years of books. 100 Monsters goes through the monsters he loved before he was 13 years old. There is a How to Write a Memoir in Three Days: A Memoir. Dave has put out over 130 ebook titles at this point. None are long. Some are wicked short. They allow a lot of different topics and styles to be used. Give some a try.

www.ingramcontent.com/pod-product-compliance
Lightning Source LLC
Chambersburg PA
CBHW021319160726
47994CB00004B/1523